WOODY GUTHRIE
Poet of the People

BONNIE CHRISTENSEN

Dragonfly Books
New York

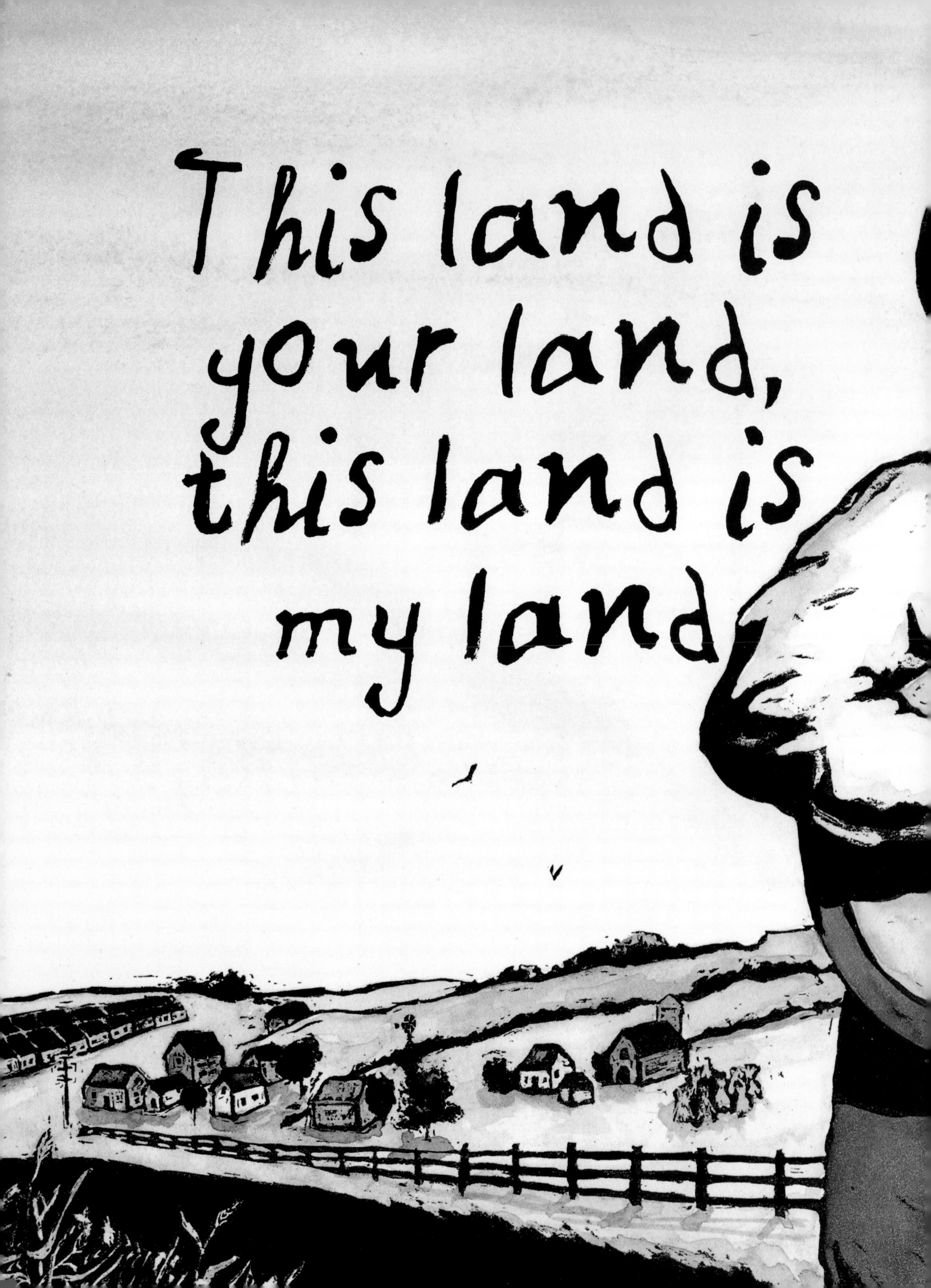
This land is
your land,
this land is
my land

This land is your land, this land is my land,
From California to the New York Island,
From the Redwood Forest, to the
    Gulf Stream waters,
This land was made for you and me.

These words, this song, are part of growing up in America. They are sung by schoolchildren and remembered by adults. The man who wrote "This Land Is Your Land" wrote more than a thousand songs. Most of them reflect the struggles and celebrate the spirit of the American people from the years of the Great Depression to today. He was the poet of the people. His name was Woody Guthrie.

Woodrow Wilson Guthrie was born in the dusty prairie town of Okemah, Oklahoma. Throughout his childhood he heard the songs that swept across the prairie—wind and rain songs, thunder rumbling, lightning crackling songs. In winter howling blizzards, in summer loud strumming of cicadas, and all through the year the crowing and neighing and grunting and bleating of farm animals. Woody was born into that music. The year was 1912.

His mother, Nora Guthrie, sang sad old country ballads in her high, twangy voice, and his father, Charley Guthrie, sang lusty tunes from his cowboy days in Texas. Woody listened.

On the Guthrie farm, young Woody listened to his father calling the pigs, a funny noise that was almost music. It made him laugh. Woody liked to make up rhymes and stories about his everyday adventures— playing war with his friends, exploring barns, climbing trees. His little stories always made his mother smile.

As Woody grew older, he spent more time in town. When he was twelve, a shoeshine man gave him a harmonica and showed him how to play. Soon Woody could echo lonesome train whistles or fast-chugging engines on his harmonica. All through the changing seasons, all along the dusty streets of town, Woody collected bits of tunes, stories, and memories. One day he would use them in his songs.

Like the seasons, the fortunes of the Guthries were changing. Woody could hear the sorrow in his father's voice as tragedies mounted and hardship became a way of life. The first and most devastating tragedy was the death of Woody's beloved older sister, Clara, in a fire. Woody was just six years old then. The whole family was overcome by grief, but Woody's mother never fully recovered. She sank into a depression, neglecting both herself and her family. As Charley Guthrie lost one job after another and finally gave up the farm, Nora Guthrie began behaving more and more oddly. Woody was fifteen when his mother was diagnosed with a "nervous disorder," which was later determined to be Huntington's disease, and hospitalized until her death two years later.

Charley Guthrie soon set off for Texas to start a new life, but Woody stayed in Okemah. Though he was small for his years, he had grown used to taking care of himself during his mother's long illness. He moved into an abandoned shack and supported himself by selling newspapers and dancing for pennies. He learned to play the Jew's harp and could squeeze a song out of bones, combs, pencils, empty bottles, or half-filled glasses of water. Those years were hard and lonesome for Woody, but he never closed his heart to others. Once when he made more money than he needed for that day's food, he gave the rest away.

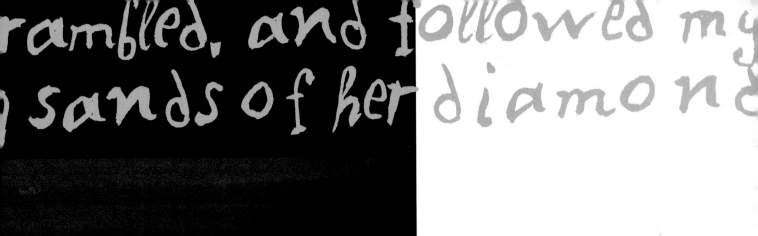

Two years later, the song of the road was loudest in Woody's head. He stuck out his thumb and hit the highway. Sometimes he rode the long, rolling freight trains with migrant workers. He liked to hang out with them in rail yards and listen to their stories and songs around the campfire.

After a summer of wandering, Woody settled with his father in an oil-boom town in west Texas. There in Pampa he learned to play guitar and started to write new words to old tunes. Before long he had formed a group called the Corncob Trio. Most young people in those days wanted to dance to the big-city sounds of jazz and swing, but Woody preferred old-time country music that got people laughing and forgetting their worries. He liked songs that could tell stories and put across ideas.

deserts, And all aro
sounding: This land w

nd me, a voice was made for you and me.

In the 1930s, there was a change in the wind. It blew hot and dry across the parched land of Oklahoma and other Great Plains states. Farm families prayed for rain, then watched as silent clouds passed without a drop. They heard the wind rattle through their withered wheat and cornfields. Every day they tasted "dust," the fine particles of soil that had blown hundreds of miles across bone-dry fields from as far north as Canada and lay in deep drifts like snow. By 1935, farmers had suffered four summers of drought. The Great Depression was hard upon them as well. Thousands of people lost their jobs as businesses and banks shut down. Farm families were evicted from their homes, their farms, their land.

When these desperate Dust Bowl farmers heard about jobs with good pay in the lush orchards of California, hundreds of thousands packed up their few belongings and headed west. Woody was one of them. And "Dusty Old Dust," the song he wrote about this great migration, says it all:

> *So long, it's been good to know ye.*
> *So long, it's been good to know ye.*
> *So long, it's been good to know ye.*
> *This dusty old dust is a-getting my home,*
> *And I've got to be drifting along.*

It was a long, hard haul from the Dust Bowl states to California, and all along the way Woody listened to the migrants' sad tales and their dreams for a better life out west. But when they reached California, the dream became a nightmare.

There were no jobs. The orchards could use only a small number of those who came. And because there was such a surplus of desperate workers, the owners of the orchards were able to pay the "lucky few" who got the jobs just a few cents a day. No matter how fast they picked the fruit or hoed the vegetables, they would never earn enough to live decently—or go back east.

While they searched for work, the homeless farm families were forced to live in crowded, unsanitary temporary camps without any schools or medical facilities. Many towns in California would not allow these families to live there at all. They were called "Okies," though most had not come from Oklahoma, and they were turned back, kicked out, moved along, and sent away.

It was clear to Woody that the people needed a voice to speak for them, a voice to ask their questions. They needed someone who was not afraid of the bosses, someone who knew what it was like to be poor.

Woody Guthrie became their voice, and songs were his way of speaking. "I . . . made up songs telling what I thought was wrong and how to make it right," he said. "Songs that said what everybody in the country was thinking."

Woody sang his Dust Bowl ballads on KFVD radio in Los Angeles on a daily program he shared with a cowgirl singer named Lefty Lou. The program brought in thousands of fan letters, more than KFVD had ever received. Some came from victims of the migration west. They were especially moved by Woody's "Talking Dust Bowl Blues" and his famous ballad "Do Re Mi" (*do re mi* is a slang expression for "money").

California is a garden of Eden,
A paradise to live in or see,
But believe it or not
You won't find it so hot,
If you ain't got the do re mi.

Woody hoped that if enough people heard how unfairly the migrant workers were being treated, then maybe everyone would get together, work for change, and make things better.

California was only one place where the people needed a voice. Woody's road stretched on and on. His people ranged from migrant field workers to coal miners to mill and factory hands. He crisscrossed America time and again, stopping in big cities and tiny towns. He talked to workers who suffered long, aching days for little pay. He

heard about illness, injury, and death on the job. Listening to the voices of the people, Woody began to believe that there was just one way individual workers could survive, and that was by joining a union. As a united group with common interests, workers could fight together for better treatment and fairer wages for each individual.

During the 1940s, Woody's songs were full of this idea. At rallies and in packed union halls, his words and music rang out. When the people joined the union, they belonged to something bigger; one person was no longer just a drop of water, but part of a powerful rushing river.

One of Woody's songs that always got workers at the rallies on their feet, cheering and joining in the rousing chorus, was "Union Maid":

> *Oh, you can't scare me, I'm sticking*
>   *to the union.*
> *I'm sticking to the union, I'm sticking*
>   *to the union.*
> *Oh, you can't scare me, I'm sticking*
>   *to the union.*
> *I'm sticking to the union till the*
>   *day I die.*

During World War II, Woody served in the Merchant Marine on ships taking troops overseas. He brought his guitar with him and used it to entertain the troops when the ship was in danger of being torpedoed by Nazi submarines. After two of his ships were hit, he decided that maybe the Army was safer and joined up.

Though Woody had never stayed in one place very long, after the war he settled in with his wife, Marjorie, and their children on Mermaid Avenue in Coney Island, New York. There his children inspired him to write silly, happy songs in which his own childlike personality shone. One of the best known was "Riding in My Car," complete with Woody's imitation of the engine and horn:

Take me riding in the car, car;
Take me riding in the car, car;
Take you riding in the car, car;
I'll take you riding in my car.

Woody would perform just about anytime, anywhere, whether in a packed auditorium with Pete Seeger and the Almanac Singers, in a New York subway station with his friend Cisco Houston, or hanging around Bryant Park

... walking my freedom ... an make me turn back.

behind the New York Public Library. He sang old songs and his own songs and songs that he made up on the spot about what was happening in the news that day. Wherever he was, he always got people involved and singing along.

this land was made for you and me.

In all Woody wrote over a thousand songs—Dust Bowl ballads, union songs, children's songs, patriotic World War II songs, songs celebrating the great beauty and power of America.

In addition he wrote hundreds of essays and newspaper articles, along with two books. He had radio shows in Los Angeles and in New York City and was recorded by the Library of Congress. His songs and ideas inspired generation after generation of singers and songwriters.

But just as Woody's songs were becoming well known and loved across the country, the tragic echoes of his childhood returned. During the 1950s, Woody's ability to perform and travel was cut short by Huntington's disease, the same illness that had killed his mother.

Eventually, Woody could no longer play his guitar or sing or even speak. But he could still listen to the wind and rain songs, the train whistling songs, the crow complaining songs. He could still hear his old friends playing familiar songs and his teenage son Arlo playing new songs.

Woody Guthrie died on October 3, 1967, but his songs live on. You can hear them in classrooms and at union rallies, on street corners, over the radio, and through open windows. Songs so familiar, so long a part of our lives, they always feel like home. Songs to tickle our funny bones. Songs to nourish our hearts, minds, souls. The music of the people.

Woody wrote this song in 1940 with seven verses. Near the end of his life he became concerned that the verses that addressed hardship and unfairness in America were often not sung. Before he died, he taught his young son Arlo all of the verses. And today the song as he intended it lives on:

THIS LAND IS YOUR LAND

*This land is your land, this land is my land
From California to the New York Island,
From the Redwood Forest, to the Gulf Stream waters,
This land was made for you and me.*

*As I went walking that ribbon of highway,
And saw above me that endless skyway,
And saw below me the golden valley, I said:
This land was made for you and me.*

*I roamed and rambled, and followed my footsteps
To the sparkling sands of her diamond deserts,
And all around me, a voice was sounding:
This land was made for you and me.*

*Was a big high wall there that tried to stop me;
A sign was painted said "Private Property."
But on the back side it didn't say nothing—
That side was made for you and me.*

*When the sun come shining, then I was strolling
In wheat fields waving, and dust clouds rolling;
The voice was chanting as the fog was lifting:
This land was made for you and me.*

*One bright sunny morning in the shadow of the steeple
By the Relief office I saw my people—
As they stood hungry, I stood there wondering if
This land was made for you and me.*

*Nobody living can ever stop me,
As I go walking my freedom highway.
Nobody living can make me turn back.
This land was made for you and me.*

Words and Music Woody Guthrie
TRO—© Copyright 1956 (Renewed) 1958 (Renewed) 1970 (Renewed)
Ludlow Music, Inc. Used by permission.

IMPORTANT EVENTS

July 14, 1912: Woodrow Wilson Guthrie is born in Okemah, Oklahoma, to Charley and Nora Guthrie.

May 1919: Woody's sister Clara dies after a fire.

1927: Woody's mother, Nora, is taken to a state mental hospital in Norman, Oklahoma.

1929: Woody leaves Oklahoma and moves to Pampa, Texas, to be with his father. His mother dies.

October 24, 1929: Black Thursday. The stock market crashes and the Great Depression begins.

1932: Woody forms the Corncob Trio with friends Matt Jennings and Cluster Baker. Promising relief from the Great Depression, Franklin D. Roosevelt is elected president. A drought strikes the Midwest, from Texas north to the Dakotas.

October 28, 1933: Woody marries Mary Jennings, sister of Matt Jennings. They will have three children, Gwendolyn Gail, Sue, and Will Rogers.

1935: In April, the Great Dust Storm hits Pampa, Texas, and other areas of the Great Plains. Woody composes his first songbook, *Alonzo M. Zilch's Own Collection of Original Songs and Ballads.* The Dust Bowl migration begins, with "Okies" moving west to California.

1936: Woody travels to California.

1937: Woody begins a new radio show with Maxine Crissman ("Lefty Lou") in Los Angeles.

1940: Woody hitchhikes to New York City and composes his first draft of "This Land Is Your Land." He records *Dust Bowl Ballads* for Victor Records and makes a series of recordings for the Library of Congress.

1941: The Bonneville Power Administration hires Woody to write songs about the Grand Coulee Dam. Woody joins the Almanac Singers and travels across the country with them, singing at union meetings.

1943: Woody and Mary are divorced. Woody publishes his autobiography, *Bound for Glory.* He joins the Merchant Marine.

1945: Woody marries Marjorie Greenblatt Mazia. They will have four children, Cathy Ann (who died at the age of four in a fire), Arlo, Joady Ben, and Nora Lee.

1952: Woody is diagnosed with Huntington's disease. Woody and Marjorie are divorced.

1953: Woody marries Anneke Van Kirk Marshall. They will have one child, Lorina Lynn.

1955: Woody and Anneke separate. Marjorie begins to take care of Woody through several stays at the Brooklyn State Hospital, Greystone Park Hospital in New Jersey, and Creedmoor State Hospital in Queens, New York.

October 3, 1967: Woody dies in Queens.

For more information about Woody Guthrie contact www.woodyguthrie.org

For Marcia

Published by
Dragonfly Books
an imprint of
Random House Children's Books
a division of Random House, Inc.
New York

THIS LAND IS YOUR LAND Words and Music by Woody Guthrie. TRO—© Copyright 1956 (Renewed) 1958 (Renewed) 1970 (Renewed) Ludlow Music, Inc., New York, NY

DUSTY OLD DUST Words and Music by Woody Guthrie. TRO—© Copyright 1940 (Renewed) 1950 (Renewed) 1963 (Renewed) Folkways Music Publishers, Inc., New York, NY

DO RE MI Words and Music by Woody Guthrie. TRO—© Copyright 1961 (Renewed) 1963 (Renewed) Ludlow Music, Inc., New York, NY

UNION MAID Words and Music by Woody Guthrie. TRO—© Copyright 1961 (Renewed) 1963 (Renewed) Ludlow Music, Inc., New York, NY

RIDING IN MY CAR Words and Music by Woody Guthrie. TRO—© Copyright 1954 (Renewed) 1969 (Renewed) Folkways Music Publishers, Inc., New York, NY

Visit us on the Web! www.randomhouse.com/kids

Educators and librarians, for a variety of teaching tools, visit us at www.randomhouse.com/teachers

The Library of Congress has cataloged the hardcover edition of this work as follows:
Christensen, Bonnie.
Woody Guthrie: poet of the people / written and illustrated by Bonnie Christensen
p.   cm.
ISBN: 978-0-375-81113-5 (trade) — ISBN: 978-0-375-91113-2 (lib. bdg.)
1. Guthrie, Woody, 1912–1967—Juvenile literature. 2. Folk singers—United States—Biography—Juvenile Literature. I. Title.
ML3930.G88 C57 2001
782.42162'13'0092—dc21
[B] 00-065504

ISBN: 978-0-553-11203-0 (pbk.)
Reprinted by arrangement with Alfred A. Knopf Books for Young Readers
Printed in China
June 2009
First Dragonfly Books Edition
10 9 8 7 6 5 4 3 2 1
All Woody Guthrie lyrics used by permission.

Random House Children's Books supports the First Amendment and celebrates the right to read.